P9-CEF-631

Letters to a Young Poet

Letters
to a
Young Poet

by
RAINER MARIA RILKE
Translated from the German by
JOAN M. BURNHAM
Foreword by
MARC ALLEN

THE CLASSIC WISDOM COLLECTION
NEW WORLD LIBRARY
SAN RAFAEL, CALIFORNIA

New World Library
58 Paul Drive
San Rafael, California 94903

© 1992 New World Library
The Classic Wisdom Collection

Translator : Joan M. Burnham
Cover design : Greg Wittrock
Text design : Nancy Benedict
Typography : Wilsted & Taylor

Library of Congress Cataloging-in-Publication Data
Rilke, Rainer Maria, 1875–1926
[Briefe an einen jungen Dichter. English]
Letters to a young poet / by Rainer Maria Rilke ;
translated from the German by Joan M. Burnham ;
introduction by Marc Allen
p.   cm.   —   (The Classic wisdom collection)
Translation of: Briefe an einen jungen Dichter.
ISBN 0-931432-94-4 (acid-free paper)
1. Rilke, Rainer Maria, 1875–1926 — Correspondence
2. Kappus, Franz Xaver, 1883–1966 — Correspondence
3. Authors, German — 20th century — Correspondence.
I. Title. II. Series.
PT2635.I65Z488 1992
831'.912 — dc20   91-42157
                                                          CIP

First printing, April 1992
Printed in the U.S.A. on acid-free paper
Distributed by Publishers Group West
12 11 10 9 8 7 6 5 4

For one human being to love another is perhaps the most difficult task of all, the epitome, the ultimate test. It is that striving for which all other striving is merely preparation.

—*Rainer Maria Rilke*

Contents

Publisher's Preface

Life is an endless cycle of change. We and our world will never remain the same.

Every generation has difficulty relating to the previous generation; even the language changes. The child speaks a different language than the parent.

It seems almost miraculous, then, that certain voices, certain books, are able to speak to not only one, but many generations beyond them. The plays and poems of William Shakespeare are still relevant today—still capable of giving us goose bumps, still entertaining, disturbing, and profound. Shakespeare is the writer who, in the English language, defines the word *classic*.

There are many other writers and thinkers who, for a great many reasons, can be considered classic, for they withstand the test of time. We want to present the best of them to you in the New World Library Classic Wisdom Collection, the thinkers who, even though they lived many years ago, are still relevant and important in today's world for the enduring words of wisdom they created, words that should forever be kept in print.

Shakti Gawain
Marc Allen
New World Library

Foreword

The ten letters that form this beautiful little book are some of the most famous letters ever written. The reason they have proven so popular over the years is that they are the work of a great soul, and they illuminate that soul; an expansive and inspiring spirit pervades them, and we are left in awe in the face of his words.

Though they were written specifically to a young poet, Rilke's words apply to everyone—especially to those who are attempting to do anything creative in their lives.

The only thing I need to add by way of introduction are the words of Franz Kappus, the young poet who received these letters: "When a truly great and unique spirit speaks, the lesser ones must be silent."

—Marc Allen

Letters to a Young Poet

Introduction

It was in the late fall of 1902. I was sitting under ancient chestnut trees, in the park of the Military Academy in the new section of Vienna, reading a book. I was so engrossed in the words that I hardly noticed when the learned and beloved chaplain of the academy, the only non-officer on the staff, Professor Horaček, seated himself beside me. He took the volume from my hands, gazed at the cover, and shook his head. "Poems of Rainer Maria Rilke?" he asked thoughtfully. He skimmed the pages, stopping now and then to scan a few verses and gaze pensively into the distance. Finally, with a nod, he said, "Well, René Rilke, my student, has turned into a poet after all."

It was then I learned about the thin, pale boy who had been sent by his parents, more than fifteen years ago, to the Military Academy to become a commissioned officer. At that time

Horaček had been chaplain there. He still remembered the former student clearly. He described him as a quiet, serious, highly gifted young man, who liked to keep to himself and who patiently endured the stress of dormitory life. After the fourth year he moved ahead with the others to the military academy in Mahrich-Weisskirchen. There, however, he apparently lacked the necessary endurance for the regimen, so his parents took him out of the school and allowed him to continue his studies at home in Prague. How the events of his life unfolded after that, Professor Horaček could not say.

After our talk, I decided to send Rainer Maria Rilke my poetic attempts and to ask him for his judgment. I was hardly twenty, not quite at the threshold of a career against which I felt an inner revolt. I hoped to receive solace and understanding, if from anyone, from the author of the book, *In Celebration of Myself*. Without actually intending it, I found myself writing letters to accompany my verses. In them I revealed my innermost self unreservedly as never before and never since to another person.

Many weeks passed before an answer to the first letter came. The blue seal revealed the postmark from Paris. It weighed heavy in my hand and revealed on the envelope the same clear, beautiful, and confident handwriting as that in the contents of the letter, from the first line to the last. Thus began my regular correspondence with Rainer Maria Rilke, which lasted until 1908. Gradually it became less frequent and finally stopped because life forced me off into paths from which the poet's gentle, warm, and touching concern would have liked to protect me.

But that is unimportant. Important alone are the ten letters—important for the understanding of the world in which Rainer Maria Rilke lived and worked, important also for the many who are growing and evolving now and shall in the future. When a truly great and unique spirit speaks, the lesser ones must be silent.

Franz Xaver Kappus
Berlin, June 1929

1

"I know of no other advice than this: Go within and scale the depths of your being from which your very life springs forth."

Paris
17 February 1903

My dear sir,

Your letter reached me just a few days ago. I want to thank you for the deep and loving trust it revealed. I can do no more. I cannot comment on the style of your verses; critical intent is too far removed from my nature. There is nothing that manages to influence a work of art less than critical words. They always result in more or less unfortunate misunderstandings. Things are not as easily understood nor as expressible as people usually would like us to believe. Most happenings are beyond expression; they exist where a word has never intruded. Even more inexpressible are works of art; mysterious entities they are, whose lives, compared to our fleeting ones, endure.

Having said these things at the outset, I now dare tell you only this: that your verses do not as yet have an individual style. Yet they possess a quiet and hidden inclination to reveal something personal. I felt that very thing most notably in the last poem, "My Soul." There, something of your inner self wants to rise to expression. And in the beautiful poem, "To Leopardi," something akin to greatness and bordering on uniqueness is sprouting out toward fulfillment. However, the poems cannot yet stand on their own merit, are not yet independent, not even the last one to Leopardi, not yet. In your kind letter accompanying them, you do not fail to admit to and to analyze some shortcomings, which I could sense while reading your verses, but could not directly put into words.

You ask whether your poems are good. You send them to publishers; you compare them with other poems; you are disturbed when certain publishers reject your attempts. Well now, since you have given me permission to advise you, I suggest that you give all that up. You are looking outward and, above all else, that you must not do now. No one can advise and help you, no one.

There is only one way: Go within. Search for the cause, find the impetus that bids you write. Put it to this test: Does it stretch out its roots in the deepest place of your heart? Can you avow that you would die if you were forbidden to write? Above all, in the most silent hour of your night, ask yourself this: *Must* I write? Dig deep into yourself for a true answer. And if it should ring its assent, if you can confidently meet this serious question with a simple, "I must," then build your life upon it. It has become your necessity. Your life, in even the most mundane and least significant hour, must become a sign, a testimony to this urge.

Then draw near to nature. Pretend you are the very first man and then write what you see and experience, what you love and lose. Do not write love poems, at least at first; they present the greatest challenge. It requires great, fully ripened power to produce something personal, something unique, when there are so many good and sometimes even brilliant renditions in great numbers. Beware of general themes. Cling to those that your everyday life offers you. Write about your sorrows, your wishes, your passing thoughts, your belief in anything beautiful. Describe all that with fervent, quiet, and humble sincerity. In order to express yourself, use things in your surroundings, the scenes of your dreams, and the subjects of your memory.

If your everyday life appears to be unworthy subject matter, do not complain to life. Complain to yourself. Lament that you are not poet enough to call up its wealth. For the creative artist there is no poverty—nothing is insignificant or unimportant. Even if you were in a prison whose walls would shut out from your senses the sounds of the outer world, would you not then still have your childhood, this precious wealth, this treasure house of memories? Direct your attention to that. Attempt to resurrect these sunken sensations of a distant past. You will gain assuredness. Your aloneness will expand and will become your home, greeting you like the quiet dawn. Outer tumult will pass it by from afar.

If, as a result of this turning inward, of this

sinking into your own world, *poetry* should emerge, you will not think to ask someone whether it is good poetry. And you will not try to interest publishers of magazines in these works. For you will hear in them your own voice; you will see in them a piece of your life, a natural possession of yours. A piece of art is good if it is born of necessity. This, its source, is its criterion; there is no other.

Therefore, my dear friend, I know of no other advice than this: Go within and scale the depths of your being from which your very life springs forth. At its source you will find the answer to the question, whether you *must* write. Accept it, however it sounds to you, without analyzing. Perhaps it will become apparent to you that you are indeed called to be a writer. Then accept that fate; bear its burden, and its grandeur, without asking for the reward, which might possibly come from without. For the creative artist must be a world of his own and must find everything within himself and in nature, to which he has betrothed himself.

It is possible that, even after your descent

into your inner self and into your secret place of solitude, you might find that you must give up becoming a poet. As I have said, to feel that one could live without writing is enough indication that, in fact, one should not. Even then this process of turning inward, upon which I beg you to embark, will not have been in vain. Your life will no doubt from then on find its own paths. That they will be good ones and rich and expansive—that I wish for you more than I can say.

What else shall I tell you? It seems to me everything has been said, with just the right emphasis. I wanted only to advise you to progress quietly and seriously in your evolvement. You could greatly interfere with that process if you look outward and expect to obtain answers from the outside—answers which only your innermost feeling in your quietest hour can perhaps give you.

I was very happy to find in your writing the name of Professor Horaček. I harbor the highest regard for this kindest of scholars and owe him lasting gratitude. Would you please pass my sentiments on to him. It is very kind of him to think of me still, and I appreciate it.

I am returning the verses with which you entrusted me. I thank you again for your unconditional and sincere trust. I am overwhelmed with it, and therefore have tried, to the best of my ability, to make myself a little more worthy than I, as a stranger to you, really am.

With my sincerest interest and devotion,
Rainer Maria Rilke

2

"We are unutterably alone, essentially, especially in the things most intimate and most important to us."

Viareggio, near Pisa, Italy
5 April 1903

You must forgive, my dear sir, that not until today could I gratefully turn my thoughts to your letter of February 24th. Until now I was not well, not exactly ill, but depressed by an influenza-type of fatigue. I was incapable of doing anything. Finally, when my situation did not seem to improve, I came to this southern seashore where I had been coaxed into well-being once before. But I am not well yet. Writing is difficult for me; therefore you must take these few lines to be more than they are.

Of course, you must know that you shall always bring me joy with each of your letters. But please have forbearance with the answers, which may well often leave you empty-handed. We are unutterably alone, essentially, especially in the things most intimate and most important to us. In order for a person to advise, even to help another, a great deal must happen. Many different elements must coincide harmoniously; a whole constellation of things must come about for that to happen even once.

I wanted to tell you about two things today:

One is about irony: Do not allow it to control you, especially during uncreative moments. In creative moments allow it to serve you as another means to better understand life. If you use it with pure intent, then it is pure. One need not be ashamed of it. But beware of a viewpoint that is too consistently ironic; turn your attention to lofty and serious issues instead. In their presence irony will pale and become helpless. Scale the depths of things; irony will never descend there. And when you are exploring thus, and arrive at the brink of greatness, ask yourself whether this ironic attitude springs from a truly deep need of your being. For due to the impact of serious things, it will either fall away from you, if it is something merely incidental, or if it truly innately belongs to you, it will be strengthened to become an important tool, and take its place with all the other instruments with which you must build your own art.

The second thing that I wanted to tell you today is this:

Of all my books there are only a few that are indispensable to me. Two of them are constantly at my fingertips wherever I may be. They are here with me now: the Bible and the books of the great Danish writer, Jens Peter Jacobsen. I wonder whether you know his works. You can obtain them easily, for some of them are published in excellent translation. Do avail yourself of the small book, *Six Stories*, by J. P. Jacobsen and his novel, *Niels Lyhne*, and begin with the first story in the first set, called "Mogens." A whole world will envelop you—the joy, the wealth, the incomprehensible greatness of a world! Live awhile within these books. Learn of them, whatever seems worth the learning, but above all, love them. For this love you shall be requited a thousand and a thousand times over, no matter what turn your life will take. This love, I am sure of it, will weave itself through the tapestry of your evolving being as one of the most important threads of your experiences, your disappointments, and your joys.

If I were obliged to tell you who taught me to experience something of the essence of creativity, the depth of it and its enduring quality, there are only two names that I can name: that of *Jacobsen*, the very greatest of writers, and *Auguste Rodin*, the sculptor. No one among all artists living today compares with them.

Success in all your ways!

Yours,
Rainer Maria Rilke

3

*"Destiny itself is like a wonderful wide
tapestry in which every thread is guided by an
unspeakably tender hand, placed beside
another thread, and held and carried by a
hundred others."*

Viareggio, near Pisa, Italy
23 April 1903

You have brought me much joy, my dear sir,
with your Easter letter, for it told me much
good about you. The way in which you expressed yourself about Jacobsen's great and
loving art showed me that I did not err in leading your life, with its many questions, to this
treasure house.

Now *Niels Lyhne*, a book of grandeur and
great depth, will reveal itself to you little by
little, the more often you read it. It seems to
contain everything, from life's most delicate
fragrance to the most full-bodied flavor of its
ripest and heaviest fruits. There is nothing in

it that would not be understandable, comprehensible, or that would not ring true to experience. There is nothing in it that would not summon a familiar resonance echoing from the memory. No experience was too insignificant—the smallest happening unfolds like destiny. Destiny itself is like a wonderful wide tapestry in which every thread is guided by an unspeakably tender hand, placed beside another thread, and held and carried by a hundred others.

You will experience the greatest happiness reading this book for the first time and will move through its countless surprises as in a new dream. And as one goes through these books later, awestruck still, they lose nothing of their wonderful power nor relinquish any of their fairy tale quality with which they overwhelmed the reader the first time.

One only becomes more and more delighted, more grateful, somehow clearer and simpler in one's perceptions. One has a deeper faith in life, is more content, and has somehow gained in self worth.

And later you must read the wonderful

book about the fate and longing of *Marie Grubbe* and Jacobsen's letters and journals and fragments, and finally, his poems. His poems live on, resounding in one's mind endlessly— even though they are only moderately well translated. In addition, I would advise you, when you have time, to buy the beautiful edition of the whole of Jacobsen's works. It contains all of these.

Concerning "Roses Should be Standing Here . . ."—this work of incomparable eloquence and form—your negative opinion of the writer of the introduction is entirely and incontestably right. Let me ask you right here to read as little as possible of aesthetic critiques. They are either prejudiced views that have become petrified and senseless in their hardened lifeless state, or they are clever word games. Their views gain approval today but not tomorrow. Works of art can be described as having an essence of eternal solitude and an understanding is attainable least of all by critique. Only love can grasp and hold them and can judge them fairly. When considering analysis, discussion, or presentation, listen to your inner

self and to your feelings every time. Should
you be mistaken, after all, the natural growth
of your inner life will guide you slowly and in
good time to other conclusions. Allow your
judgments their own quiet, undisturbed devel-
opment, which, as with all progress, must
come from deep within and can in no way be
forced or hastened. *All things* consist of carrying to term and then giving birth. To allow the
completion of every impression, every germ of
a feeling deep within, in darkness, beyond
words, in the realm of instinct unattainable by
logic, to await humbly and patiently the hour
of the descent of a new clarity: that alone is to
live one's art, in the realm of understanding as
in that of creativity.

In this there is no measuring with time. A
year doesn't matter; ten years are nothing. To
be an artist means not to compute or count;
it means to ripen as the tree, which does
not force its sap, but stands unshaken in the
storms of spring with no fear that summer
might not follow. It will come regardless. But
it comes only to those who live as though eternity stretches before them, carefree, silent,

and endless. I learn it daily, learn it with many pains, for which I am grateful: *Patience* is all!

My reaction to the books of Richard Dehmel—the same, by the way, as to the person, whom I do know slightly—is this: When I have found one of his well-written beautiful pages, I am then already afraid of the next ones, which destroy everything again and can turn that which is worthy of love into something unworthy. You have characterized him very well with the words, "lustful in his life and writing." Actually the creative experience lies so unbelievably close to the sexual, close to its pain and its pleasure, that both phenomena are only different forms of the same longing and bliss. If one could say "sexuality" instead of "lust"—sexuality in a large sense, in a wide pure sense, not one suspect by the church, then his art would be great and infinitely important. His poetic talent is great and as strong as the primeval urge; it has an impetuous rhythm that breaks forth out of him as water out of the rocks.

But it seems that this power of his is not always entirely genuine and not without assuming a pose. (After all, this is indeed one of the most difficult tests for the true artist: he must always remain innocently unaware of his best virtues if he does not wish to rob them of their spontaneity and their unaffectedness.) And when Dehmel's creative power, rushing through his being, meets the sexual, then it finds the man not quite so pure as he needs to be. For him there exists no totally mature and pure world of sex, none that is simply human and not *masculine* only. For him there exists lust, intoxication, and restlessness, beleaguered with the old prejudices and pride, with which the male has disfigured and burdened love. He loves only as *male*, not simply as a human being. Consequently there is in his perception something confining, something spiteful, seemingly wild, something temporal, not eternal. There is something that detracts from his art, and makes it suggestive and questionable. His art is not without blemish; it has been imprinted with passion and transience. Little of it will continue and endure. (But this is true of most art.)

In spite of that, one can appreciate and enjoy the part that is great. One must simply not be overwhelmed nor become a partisan to Dehmel's world, which is so infinitely fearful, full of adultery and confusion, far from the true destinies of man. They may on the one hand cause more real suffering than his fleeting gloom, but will also offer more opportunities for greatness and more courage for eternity.

Finally, regarding my books, I wish I could send you all of those that would somehow give you pleasure. However, I am very poor and my books, as soon as they are published, no longer belong to me. I can't even afford them myself, and, as I would often like, give them to those who would consider it a gift of love.

So I will write the titles and publishers of my most recent books on another piece of paper. (Of the newest ones published, there must be twelve or thirteen.) I must leave it up to you to order some of my works some time at your convenience.

I am happy to know my books will be with you.

Goodby for now!

Yours,
Rainer Maria Rilke

4

"If you will stay close to nature, to its simplicity, to the small things hardly noticeable, those things can unexpectedly become great and immeasurable."

Worpswede near Bremen
16 July 1903

About ten days ago I left Paris, suffering and tired, and rode into a large northern plain. Its expanse, its quiet, and its sky are to restore my health. But I entered the region during a long rain that has not until today let up a bit over this restless drifting land. I am using this first moment of brightness to greet you, dear friend.

My dear Mr. Kappus, I have had a letter of yours here for a long time, awaiting my answer. Not that I had forgotten it; to the contrary, it is the kind that one reads again, when one finds it among others. I singled yours out to read, and you seemed so very near. It was the letter of May 2nd; you surely remember it. When I read it, as I am doing now, in the immense silence of this distant land, your beautiful concern about life touches me even more than it did in Paris, where everything seems strange, and one's impressions seem to tremble and fade into the terrible noise all around. Here, surrounded by a powerful land, over which the winds travel from the seas, here I feel that no man can answer those questions of yours and explain those feelings that in their depths have a life of their own. Even the best writers can err in their expressions when they are asked to interpret the faintest of impulses and that which is beyond words.

Nevertheless, I do believe you need not be left without answers, if you will cling to things resembling those that are now rejuvenating me. If you will stay close to nature, to its simplicity, to the small things hardly noticeable, those things can unexpectedly become great and immeasurable. If you will love what seems to be insignificant and will in an unassuming manner, as a servant, seek to win the

confidence of what seems poor, then everything will become easier, more harmonious,
and somehow more conciliatory, not for your
intellect—that will most likely remain behind, astonished—but for your innermost
consciousness, your awakeness, and your inner knowing.

You are so young; you stand before begin-
nings. I would like to beg of you, dear friend,
as well as I can, to have patience with everything that remains unsolved in your heart. Try
to love the *questions themselves*, like locked
rooms and like books written in a foreign language. Do not now look for the answers. They
cannot now be given to you because you could
not live them. It is a question of experiencing
everything. At present you need to *live* the
question. Perhaps you will gradually, without
even noticing it, find yourself experiencing the
answer, some distant day. Perhaps you are indeed carrying within yourself the potential to
visualize, to design, and to create for yourself
an utterly satisfying, joyful, and pure life-
style. Discipline yourself to attain it, but

accept that which comes to you with deep trust, and as long as it comes from your own will, from your own inner need, accept it, and do not hate anything.

To cope with sexuality is difficult. Yes, but everything assigned to us is a challenge; nearly everything that matters is a challenge, and everything matters. If you would only recognize that and come to the place where you would strive on your own to finally gain your very own relationship with sexuality, always keeping aware of *your* native bent and *your* personality, your *own* experience, your childhood, and your strengths, then you need no longer fear losing yourself and becoming unworthy of your sexuality, your most precious possession.

Physical lust is a sensuous experience no different from innocently viewing something, or from the feeling of pure delight when a wonderful ripe fruit fills the tongue. It is a glorious infinite experience granted us, a gift of knowledge from the world, the fullness and radiance of all knowing. It is not bad that we welcome it.

What is bad is that almost all misuse and waste it. They set it out as a lure in dreary places of their lives and use it as a distraction rather than as a focus on great heights.

Man has also transformed eating into something else. Lack on the one hand and excess on the other have clouded the clarity of this basic need. Similarly cloudy have become all the deep and simple human needs in which life renews itself. But the individual can clarify them for himself and can live that clarity—as long as he is not too dependent on others, as long as he has a pact with aloneness.

We can recall that all beauty in animals and plants is a silent and enduring form of love and longing. We can see the animal just as we perceive the plant, patiently and willingly uniting, multiplying, and growing, not from physical desire, not from physical grief, rather from adapting to what has to be. That existing order transcends desire and grief and is mightier than will and resistance. The earth is full of this secret down to her smallest things. Oh, that we would only receive this secret more humbly, bear it more earnestly, endure it, and feel how awesomely difficult it is, rather than to take it lightly.

Oh, that we might hold in reverence our fertility, which is but *one*, even if it seems to be either spiritual or physical. Spiritual creativity originates from the physical. They are of the same essence—only spiritual creativity is a gentler, more blissful, and more enduring repetition of physical desire and satisfaction. The desire to be a creator, to give birth, to guide the growth process is nothing without its constant materialization in the world, nothing without the thousandfold consent of things and animals. Its enjoyment is so indescribably beautiful and rich only because it is filled with inherited memories of millions of instances of procreation and births. In one thought of procreation a thousand forgotten nights of love are resurrected and that thought is fulfilled in grandeur and sublimity. They who meet in the night to be entwined and sway in passionate lust are performing a serious work. They are gathering "sweets" and depth and power for the song of some future poet, who shall arise and speak of unspeakable bliss. They beg the future to wait to become the present, and they blindly embrace, believing their wish. Even so, they are mistaken. The future does come; a new human being arises, due to the law of nature. A strong resistant seed forces itself to the ovum that draws it willingly to itself.

Do not allow yourself to be misled by the surfaces of things. In the great depths all becomes law. They who live this mystery badly and ineffectually (and there are many), lose it only for themselves. Even so, they pass it on like a sealed letter without knowing it. Do not be misled by the great number of names and the complexity of cases. Perhaps there is over all a great motherhood expressed as mutual longing.

The beauty of a virgin, a being that, as you so aptly say, has not yet accomplished anything, is motherhood having a presentiment of itself, is in preparation, and has fears and longings. The beauty of the mother is that of a serving motherhood. And within the aged one there dwells an awesome memory.

Within the man, motherhood exists also, it seems to me, both physical and spiritual. His part in procreation is also a type of giving birth, and giving birth it is when he draws strength from his innermost abundance.

Perhaps the sexes are more closely related than one would think. Perhaps the great renewal of the world will consist of this, that man and woman, freed of all confused feelings and desires, shall no longer seek each other as opposites, but simply as members of a family and neighbors, and will unite as *human beings*, in order to simply, earnestly, patiently, and jointly bear the heavy responsibility of sexuality that has been entrusted to them.

But he who has a pact with aloneness can even now prepare the way for all of this that in the future may well be possible for many, and can build with hands less apt to err. Therefore, dear friend, embrace your solitude and love it. Endure the pain it causes, and try to sing out with it. For those near to you are distant, you say. That shows it is beginning to dawn around you; there is an expanse opening about you. And when your nearness becomes distant, then you have already expanded far: to being among the stars. Your horizon has widened greatly. Rejoice in your growth. No one can join you in that.

Be good to those who stay behind, and be quiet and confident in their presence. Do not torment them with your doubts, and do not shock them with your confidence or your joy, which they cannot understand. Try to establish with them a simple, sincere mutual feeling of communion, that need not change if you yourself change. Love the life that is theirs, although different from yours. Be considerate of aging persons, for they fear the very aloneness in which you place your trust. Avoid adding substance to those dramas always unleashed between parents and children. These encounters cause the children to expend much energy and consumes the love of their elders. Even so, their love is warm, and has its effect, although it does not understand. Believe, however, in a love that will be safely kept for you as a legacy and a trust, and trust that

41

in it there is a power and a blessing. You do not have to leave its presence in order to make very great strides ahead.

It is good that you are settling into a career that will make you independent, and that you will be relying completely on yourself in every sense. Wait patiently to see if your inner life feels restricted by the conditions of this career. I take it to be very difficult and very demanding, since it is burdened with many conventions, hardly allowing your personal interpretation of its designated duties. However, your pact with aloneness will be your support and solace even in the midst of unfamiliar situations. It is through that aloneness that you will find all your paths. All my wishes are prepared to accompany you, and so will my trust in you.

Yours,
Rainer Maria Rilke

5

"There is much beauty here because there is much beauty everywhere."

Rome
29 October 1903

My dear sir,

I received your letter of August 29th in Florence and not until now, after two months, am I letting you know it. Please excuse this belatedness. I do dislike writing letters when traveling because I need more than the basic writing implements: I need quiet and solitude and at least one friendly hour.

We arrived in Rome about six weeks ago, at a time when it was still empty, hot, and notoriously feverish. This condition, along with other mundane difficulties with accommodations, contributed to the unrest around us that seemed not to want to end, and to the strangeness of our surroundings and our temporary homelessness. Rome, if one does not know the city, can be depressingly sad for the first few

45

days. It affected me so, because it exudes a death-like, dreary atmosphere, typical of museums. The over-abundant relics of the past have been resurrected and their revival maintained with tremendous effort. From them a very small segment presently makes its living. All of these distorted and stale things are basically nothing more than coincidental remnants of another era and another kind of life, which is not ours and should not be considered as our own. They have been indiscriminately overrated by many, including scholars and philologists and tourists, who habitually travel to Italy.

Finally, after weeks of daily resistance, one finds himself somewhat composed again, even if still a bit confused. One says to himself: No, there is not *more* beauty here than elsewhere. All these things have been restored and improved by the work of craftsmen. They have been and are admired and revered by generations past and present, and that will continue into the future. All these things mean nothing, are nothing, and have no heart, no worth. Yet there is much beauty here.

There is much beauty here because there is

much beauty everywhere. Unending streams of lively water flow over the old aqueducts in the large city. They dance in the city squares over white stone bowls and spread themselves out in wide roomy basins. They rustle by day and raise their voice to the night. Night here is grand, expansive, soft from the winds, and full of stars. And gardens are here, unforgettable avenues lined with trees. And staircases are here, steps conceived by Michelangelo, steps that were modeled after downward gliding waters, broad in their descent, one step giving birth to another, as wave from wave. Through such impressions one composes himself and wins himself back from the demands of the multiplicities that speak and chatter. (How very talkative they are!) One gradually learns to recognize the very few things in which eternity dwells, which one can love, and solitude, of which one can softly partake.

I still reside in the city, at the Capitol, not far from the most beautiful sculpture of horse and rider that has been preserved for us from Roman art—that of Marcus Aurelius. However, in a few weeks I shall move to a quiet, modest room, an old summerhouse that lies lost deep in a large park, hidden from the noise and applause of the city. There I shall live the whole winter and shall enjoy the great silence. I expect it will give me the gift of pleasant times and hours of accomplishment. . . .

From there, where I shall feel more at home, I shall write you a longer letter and shall include the subject of your writing. Today I must tell you only this (perhaps it is not right that I did not do it sooner), that the book mentioned in your letter, which was to have contained work of yours, has not arrived here. Has it perhaps been returned to you, perhaps from Worpswede? For packages sent to a foreign country are not forwarded. This possibility is the most likely and I would appreciate a confirmation. I hope it does not mean a loss to you. I regret to say that in Italy this kind of situation is not unusual.

I would gladly have received this book, as is true of everything that pertains to you. Verses that you have meanwhile composed— if you entrust them to me—I shall always read, reread, and experience as well and as sincerely as I can.

     With best wishes and greetings,
      Yours,
      Rainer Maria Rilke

6

"Reflect on the world that you carry within yourself. And name this thinking what you wish. . . . Your innermost happening is worth all your love."

Rome
23 December 1903

My dear Mr. Kappus,

You should not be without a greeting from me at Christmastime, when in the midst of the festivities your feeling of aloneness is apt to weigh more heavily upon you. Whenever you notice that it looms large, then be glad about it. For what would aloneness be, you ask yourself, if it did not possess greatness? There exists only *one* aloneness, and it is *great*, and it is not easy to bear. To nearly everyone come those hours that we would gladly exchange for any cheap or even the most banal camaraderie, for even the slightest inclination to choose the second-best or the most unworthy thing. But perhaps it is exactly in those hours when aloneness can flourish. Its growth is painful as the growing up of a young boy and sad as the emergence of springtime.

But that should not confuse you. What you really need is simply this—aloneness, great inner solitude. To go within and for hours not to meet anyone—that is what one needs to attain. To be lonely as one was lonely as a child, while adults were moving about, entangled with things that seemed big and important, because the grownups looked so officious and because one could not understand any of their doings—that must be the goal. And when you realize one day that their activities are superficial, that their careers are paralyzed and no longer linked with life, then why not look at the world as a child would see it—out of the depths of your own world, out of the breadth of your own aloneness, which is itself work and rank and career? Why should anyone wish to exchange a child's wise incomprehension for resistance and disdain, since the incomprehension *is* aloneness, and resistance and disdain are an involvement in the things you seek to escape from.

Think, dear friend, reflect on the world that you carry within yourself. And name this thinking what you wish. It might be recollections of your childhood or yearning for your own future. Just be sure that you observe carefully what wells up within you and place that above everything that you notice around you. Your innermost happening is worth all your love. You must somehow work on that.

Do not expend too much courage or time to clarify your position to others. I know your career is difficult and I anticipated your complaint and knew it would come. Now that it has come, I cannot reassure you. I can only advise you to think seriously about this: Are not all careers the same, filled with demands and people filled with animosity toward the individual, at the same time absorbing the hatred of those who have silently and sullenly adapted to dull duty? The situation that you are now obliged to tolerate is not burdened any heavier with conventions, prejudices, and errors than any other situation. If there are some who outwardly give the impression of granting more freedom, know that there really exists none that is related to the important things that make up real life. The individual person who senses his aloneness, and only he, is like a thing subject to the deep laws, the cosmic laws. If a person goes out into the dawn or gazes out into the evening filled with happenings, if he senses what happens there, then all situations fall away from him as from someone dead, even though he stands in the midst of life.

You, dear Mr. Kappus, as an officer in the military, need to experience this feeling. You must realize that you would have felt the same way in any existing career now. Yes, aside from that, independent of career, if you had sought connections in society, you would not have been spared this feeling of constraint. It is the same everywhere, but that is not a reason for fear or sadness. If there seems to be no communication between you and the people around you, try to draw close to those things that will not ever leave you. The nights are still there and the winds that roam through the trees and over many lands. Amidst things and among animals are happenings in which *you* can participate. The children too, are still the same as you were as a child, sad and happy in the same way. And if you think about your childhood, then you can again live among them, the lonely children—where the adults count for nothing and their dignity has no worth.

And if it is distressing and agonizing for you to think of your childhood and of the simplicity and silence so close akin to it, because you no longer believe in God, who is constantly appearing there, then ask yourself, dear Mr. Kappus, whether you have really lost God. Is it not rather true that you have not yet possessed him? For when could that have been? Do you think a child can hold him, him whom men can bear only with great effort and whose weight crushes the aged ones? Do you think that the one possessing him could lose him like a little stone? Or do you not rather agree that he who might have him could be lost *by him?* However, if you conclude that he did not exist in your childhood and not before that, if you surmise that Christ was deluded by his yearning and that Mohammed was betrayed by his pride—and if you, with great dismay, feel that he does not exist, even during this hour, while we are speaking of him, what right have you then to miss him, like someone out of the past, him, who never existed, and to seek him as though he were lost?

Why don't you think of him as the coming one, who has been at hand since eternity, the future one, the final fruit of a tree, with us as its leaves? What is keeping you from hurling his birth into evolving times and from living your life as though it were one painful beautiful day in the history of a great pregnancy? Don't you see that everything that happens becomes a beginning again and again? Could it not be *His* beginning, since a beginning in itself is always so beautiful? If, however, he is the most perfect one, would not what is less than perfect have to precede him, so that he can choose himself from great abundance? Would not *He* have to be the last one, in order to envelop everything within himself? And what sense would our existence make, if the one we longed for had already had his existence in the past?

By extracting the most possible sweetness out of everything, just as the bees gather honey, we thus build Him. With any insignificant thing, even with the very smallest thing—if only it is done out of love—we begin, with work, with a time of rest following, with keeping silent or with a small lonely joy, with everything that we do alone, without participants or supporters, we begin Him: the one whom we shall not experience in this lifetime, even as our ancestors could not experience us. Yet they who belong to the distant past are in us, serving as impetus, as a burden to our fate, as blood that can be heard rushing, as a gesture rising out of the depths of time.

Is there anything now that can rob you of the hope of someday being in Him, who is the ultimate, in the infinite future, as once He was in your past?

Celebrate Christmas, dear Mr. Kappus, with this *reverent* feeling that He perhaps needs exactly this, your fear of life, in order to begin. Perhaps these very days of your transition are the times that He is touched by everything within you. Perhaps you are influencing him, just as you as a child with breathless effort left your mark on Him. Be patient and without rancor and believe that the least we can do is to make His evolving no more difficult than the earth does for spring, when it wishes to come.

Be glad and comforted,
Yours,
Rainer Maria Rilke

7

"We must embrace struggle. Every living thing conforms to it. Everything in nature grows and struggles in its own way, establishing its own identity, insisting on it at all cost, against all resistance."

Rome
14 May 1904

My dear Mr. Kappus,

Much time has elapsed since I received your last letter. Do not hold it against me. First it was work, then interruptions, and finally illness that over and over again kept me from responding. I did so wish it to come out of quiet and good days. Now I feel a bit better. The beginning of spring with its nasty and changeable moods was present here too, unmistakably so. And now I am finally able to greet you (which I do so very gladly) and to respond with one thing and another to your letter, as well as I can.

I have copied your sonnet because I found

it beautiful and simple and well suited to the form in which it moves so naturally, with quiet proper decorum. It is the best of your verses that I have had the privilege to read. And now I shall give you my copy of them, for I know that it is important and also a new experience to find one's own work again in someone else's handwriting. Read these verses as though you had never seen them before, and you will feel in your innermost being how very much they are your own.

It was a joy for me to read this sonnet and your letter often. I thank you for both.

Do not allow yourself to be confused in your aloneness by the something within you that wishes to be released from it. This very wish, if you will calmly and deliberately use it as a tool, will help to expand your solitude into far distant realms. People have, with the help of so many conventions, resolved everything the easy way, on the easiest side of easy. But it is clear that we must embrace struggle. Every living thing conforms to it. Everything in nature grows and struggles in its own way, establishing its own identity, insisting on it at all cost, against all resistance. We can be sure of very little, but the need to court struggle is a surety that will not leave us. It is good to be lonely, for being alone is not easy. The fact that something is difficult must be one more reason to do it.

To love is also good, for love is difficult. For one human being to love another is perhaps the most difficult task of all, the epitome, the ultimate test. It is that striving for which all other striving is merely preparation. For that reason young people—who are beginners in everything—cannot yet love; they do not know how to love. They must learn it. With their whole being, with all strengths enveloping their lonely, disquieted heart, they must learn to love—even while their heartbeat is quickening. However, the process of learning always involves time set aside for solitude. Thus to love constantly and far into a lifespan is indeed aloneness, heightened and deepened aloneness for one who loves.

Love does not at first have anything to do with arousal, surrender, and uniting with another being—for what union can be built upon uncertainty, immaturity, and lack of coherence? Love is a high inducement for individuals to ripen, to strive to mature in the inner self, to manifest maturity in the outer world, to become that manifestation for the sake of another. This is a great, demanding task; it calls one to expand one's horizon greatly. Only in this sense, as the task to work on themselves, day and night, and to listen, ought young people use the love granted them. Opening one's self, and surrendering, and every kind of communion is not for them yet; they must for a very, very long time gather and harbor experience. It is the final goal, perhaps one which human beings as yet hardly ever seek to attain.

Young people often err, and that intensely so, in this way, since it is their nature to be impatient: They throw themselves at each other when loves comes upon them. They fragment themselves, just as they are, in all of their disarray and confusion. But what is to follow? What should fate do if this takes root, this heap of half-broken things that they call togetherness and that they would like to call their happiness?

What of their future? Everyone loses himself for the sake of the other and loses the other and many others that would yet have wished to come. They lose perspective and limit opportunities. They exchange the softly advancing and retreating of gentle premonitions of the spirit for an unfruitful restlessness. Nothing can come of it; nothing, that is, but disappointment, poverty, and escape into one of the many conventions that have been put up in great numbers, like public shelters, on this most dangerous road. No area of human experience is provided with as many conventions as this one: there are flotation devices of the most unusual sort; there are boats and life belts. Society has known how to create every kind of refuge conceivable. Since it is inclined to perceive love life as entertainment, it needs to display it as easily available, inexpensive, safe, and reliable, just like common public entertainment.

It is true that many young people who do

not love rightly, who simply surrender themselves and leave no room for aloneness, experience the depressing feeling of failure. They
would, in their own personal way, like to turn
the condition in which they find themselves
into something meaningful and fruitful. Their
nature tells them that questions of love can be
solved even less easily than everything else
usually considered important, and certainly
not publicly or by this or that agreement.
Questions of love are personal, intimate questions, from one person to another, that in
every case require a new, a special, and an *ex-
clusively* personal answer. But then, having
already thrown themselves together, having
set no boundaries between each other, and
being no longer able to differentiate, they no
longer possess anything of their own. How can
they on their own find the escape route that
they have already blocked to that inner solitude?

They act from a source of mutual helplessness. If, with the best of intentions, they wish
to avoid the convention that is approaching

them (marriage, for example) they find themselves in the clutches of another conventional solution, one less obvious, but just as deadly. Everything surrounding them, spread wide about them, is—convention. There, where a dull mutuality, prematurely established, is the basis for living, *every* action is conventional. Every situation leading to such confusion has its convention, be it ever so unusual, that is, in the ordinary sense, immoral. Yes, even separation would be a conventional step, an impersonal, coincidental decision, a weak and fruitless decision. Whoever will seriously consider the question of love will find that, as with the question of death, difficult as it is, there is no enlightened answer, no solution, not the hint of a path has yet been found. And for these two deep concerns that we carry safely disguised within us and that we pass on unresolved, for them no comforting principle will be learned, none finding general agreement.

But to the same degree that we as individuals begin to explore life, to that degree shall these deep things surface for each of us in greater intimacy. The responsibility that the difficult work of love demands of our evolvement overwhelms us; it is larger than life. We, as yet beginners, are not equal to it. If we persevere after all, and take this love upon us, accepting it as a burden and a time of training, instead of losing ourselves to the frivolous and careless game behind which people have hidden themselves, not willing to face the most serious question of their being—then perhaps shall a small bit of progress be perceptible as well as some relief for those to come after us. That would be a great deal.

We are just now reaching the point where we can observe objectively and without judgment the relationship of one individual to a second one. Our attempts to live such a relationship are without a model. Yet, there already exists within our time frame some things intended to help our faint-hearted beginner's steps. The girl and the woman in their own new unfolding will only temporarily be imitators of male incivilities, of men's ways, and repeaters of men's careers. After the insecurity of this transition has passed, it will be shown that women, through their wealth of (often ridiculous) disguises and many changes, have continued their quest only in order to purify their own beings of the distorting influences of the other sex. The women, within whom life dwells in a more direct, fruitful, and trusting way, must, after all, have become basically more mature, more human than the man. For he is easily pulled down by the weight of the lack of physical fruitfulness, pulled down under the surface of life; he professes to love that which he arrogantly and rashly underrates.

The simple humanity of woman, brought about through pain and abasement, shall then come to light when the convention of her ultra-feminism will have been stripped off, transforming her status in the world. The men, who today cannot yet feel it coming, shall be surprised and defeated by it. One day (in northern countries trustworthy signs can already be seen and heard), the girl and the woman shall exist with her name no longer contrasted to the masculine; it shall have

71

a meaning in itself. It shall not bring to mind complement or limitation—only life and being: the feminine human being.

This progress shall transform the experience of love, presently full of error, opposed at first by men, who have been overtaken in their progress by women. It shall thoroughly change the love experience to the rebuilding of a relationship meant to be between two persons, no longer just between man and woman. And this more human love will be consummated, endlessly considerate and gentle, good and clear in its bonding and releasing; it shall resemble that love for which we must prepare painstakingly and with fervor, which will be comprised of two lonelinesses protecting one another, setting limits, and acknowledging one another.

And one more thing: Do not believe that this idea of a great love, which, when you were a boy, was imposed upon you, has been lost. Can you not say that since then great and good wishes have ripened within you, and resolutions too, by which you live today? I believe that this idea of love remains so strong and mighty in your memory because it was your first deep experience of aloneness and the first inner work that you have done on your life.

All good wishes for you, dear Mr. Kappus.

Yours,

Rainer Maria Rilke

8

"How could we be capable of forgetting the old myths that stand at the threshold of all mankind, myths of dragons transforming themselves at the last moment into princesses? Perhaps all dragons in our lives are really princesses just waiting to see us just once being beautiful and courageous."

Borgeby gård, Flädie, Sweden
12 August 1904

I want to talk to you again for a little while, dear Mr. Kappus, even though I have hardly anything helpful to say—hardly anything useful. You have encountered many very sad experiences, which by now have passed. You say that even their passing was difficult and depressing. Please, dear friend, think about this: Did not this great sadness rather pass through you? Did not much within you change? Did you not, somehow at some place in your being, change while you were sad? The only sad experiences which are dangerous and bad are those that one reveals to people in order to drown them out. Like illnesses treated superficially and incompetently, they retreat and, after a short pause, break out even more intensely. They gather together within the self and are life. They are life unlived, ridiculed and scorned.

Were it possible, we might look beyond the reach of our knowing and yet a bit further into the past across the farmsteads of our ancestors. Then perhaps we would endure our griefs with even greater trust than our joys. For they are the moments when something new has entered into us, something unfamiliar. Our feelings become mute in timid shyness. Everything within us steps back; a silence ensues, and the something new, known to no one, stands in the center and is silent.

I believe that nearly all our griefs are moments of tension. We perceive them as crippling because we no longer hear signs of life from our estranged emotions. We are alone with the strange thing that has stepped into our presence. For a moment everything intimate and familiar has been taken from us. We stand in the midst of a transition, where we cannot remain standing.

And this is the reason the sadness passes: the something new within us, the thing that has joined us, has entered our heart, has gone into its innermost chamber and is no longer there either—it is already in the blood. And we do not find out what it was. One could easily make us believe that nothing happened; and yet we have been changed, as a house is changed when a guest has entered it. We cannot say who came; we shall perhaps never know. But many signals affirm that the future has stepped into us in such a way as to change itself into us, and that long before it manifests itself outwardly.

Therefore it is so important to be alone and observant when one is sad. The seemingly uneventful moment, when our future really enters in, is very much closer to reality than that other loud and fortuitous point in time, when it happens as if coming from the outside. The quieter and more patient, the more open we are when we are sad, the more resolutely does that something new enter into us, the deeper it is absorbed in us, the more certain we are to secure it, and the more certain it is to become our *personal* destiny. When it "happens" at a later time—when it becomes obvious to others—then we feel an intimate kinship with it. And that is necessary. It is needed, and our evolvement will gradually go in that direction: nothing strange shall befall us, but rather that which has already for a long time belonged to us.

We have already had to rethink so many concepts about movement. Surely it is possible that we shall gradually learn to recognize that what we call fate emerges *from* human beings; it does not enter into them from the outside. It is only because so many did not absorb their destinies while they lived in them, did not transform them into themselves, that they did not recognize what emerged from them. Their fate was so strange to them that in their confused fright they believed it must just now have entered into them. For they swore never before to have found anything similar within themselves. As people were mistaken so long about the movement of the sun, so it is that people are yet mistaken about the movement of what is to come. The future stands firm and still, my dear Franz, but we are moving in infinite space.

Why should we not encounter difficulties?

To return to the subject of aloneness: It becomes increasingly clear that it is basically not something we can choose to have or not to have. We simply *are* alone. One can only delude one's self and act as though it were not so—that is all. How much better, however, that we concede we are solitary beings; yes, that we assume it to be true. Our minds will certainly reel at the thought, for all points on which we could heretofore focus shall be taken from us. There is nothing near and familiar left us; everything is in the distance, unendingly far away.

A person would have a similar feeling, were he, with practically no preparation or transition, taken from his home and placed on the summit of a high mountain. It would be a feeling of unequaled uncertainty—a vulnerability to a nameless something would nearly destroy him. He would think he were falling or would believe himself flung out into space or burst asunder into a thousand pieces. What a colossal lie his mind would have to invent to catch up with the condition of his senses and to clarify it. That is how all sense of distance, all measurements change for the one who is alone.

Some of these changes cause many to lose all perspective. And, as with the man on the pinnacle of the mountain, unusual imaginings emerge and strange sensations arise that seem to grow beyond everything endurable. But it is necessary that we experience *that* also. We must accept our existence *to the greatest extent possible;* everything, the unprecedented also, needs to be accepted. That is basically the only case of courage required of us: to be courageous in the face of the strangest, the most whimsical and unexplainable thing that we could encounter.

The fact that people have been cowards in that regard has caused infinite harm to life. The experiences that one calls "ghosts," the entire spirit world, death, all these related things have been forced out of life through daily resistance to such an extent that the senses with which we could grasp them have become atrophied. And that is not even considering the question of God.

The fear of the unexplainable impoverished not only the existence of the individual, but also caused the relationship of one person to another to be limited. It is as though fear has caused something to be lifted out of the riverbed of limitless possibilities to a fallow stretch of shore where nothing happens. For it is not inertia alone that causes the unspeakably monotonous and unrenewed human condition to repeat itself again and again. It is the aversion to anything new, any unpredictable experience, which is believed to be untenable.

Only he who can expect anything, who does not exclude even the mysterious, will have a relationship to life greater than just being alive; he will exhaust his own wellspring of being. If we liken the existence of the individual to a room of larger or smaller size, it is evident that most people are familiar with only a corner of their room, perhaps a window seat or space where they pace to and fro. In that way they have a certain security. Yet every uncertainty fraught with danger is so much more human. It is the same uncertainty that motivated the prisoners in Edgar Allen Poe's stories to explore the form of their terrible prisons and not to be a stranger to the unspeakable horrors of their presence there.

But we are not prisoners. There are no traps or snares set for us, and there is nothing that should frighten or torture us. We are placed into life, into the element best suited to it. Besides, through thousands of years of adaptation, we have acquired such a resemblance to this life, that we, if we stood still, would hardly be distinguishable from our surroundings. We have no reason to mistrust our world, for it is not against us. If it has terrors, they are *our own* terrors. If it has precipices, they belong to us. If dangers are present, we must try to love them. And if we fashion our life according to that principle, which advises us to embrace that which is difficult, then that which appears to us to be the very strangest will become the most worthy of our trust, and the truest.

How could we be capable of forgetting the old myths that stand at the threshold of all mankind, myths of dragons transforming themselves at the last moment into princesses? Perhaps all dragons in our lives are really princesses just waiting to see us just once being beautiful and courageous. Perhaps everything fearful is basically helplessness that seeks our help.

You must not be frightened, dear Mr. Kappus, when a sadness arises within you of such magnitude as you have never experienced, or when a restlessness overshadows all you do, like light and the shadow of clouds gliding over your hand. You must believe that something is happening to you, that life has not forgotten you, that it holds you in its hand. It shall not let you fall.

Why should you want to exclude any anxiety, any grief, any melancholy from your life, since you do not know what it is that these conditions are accomplishing in you? Why do you want to persecute yourself with the question of where everything comes from and where it is headed? You do know that you are in a period of transition and wish for nothing as much as to transform yourself. If some aspect of your life is not well, then consider the illness to be the means for an organism to free itself from something foreign to it. In that case you must help it to be ill and to have its whole illness, to let it break out. That is the course of its progress.

So much is happening within you at present, dear Mr. Kappus. You need to be as patient as someone ill and as optimistic as one recuperating, for perhaps you are both. And more: You are also the physician who must watch over yourself. But in the course of every illness there are many days in which the physician can do nothing but wait. And that, above all, to the extent that you are your physician, you must do now.

Do not scrutinize yourself too closely. Do not draw conclusions too quickly from that which is happening to you. Just allow it to happen. Otherwise you might easily begin to look with blame (that is, morally speaking) upon your past, which, of course, is very much a part of everything that you encounter now.

The influences of the vagaries, the wishes and
the longings of your boyhood upon your present life are not the ones you remember or pass
judgment on. The unusual conditions of a
lonely and helpless childhood are so difficult,
so complicated, vulnerable to so many influences, and at the same time so distant from all
real connections with life, that, whenever a
vice may have entered, one may not simply
call it a vice. One must, in any case, be very
careful with that nomenclature. It is often the
name of the crime upon which a life shatters,
not the nameless and personal act itself at all.
It might have been a definite necessity of this
person's life, of which he may simply have
availed himself.

The expending of effort seems so important to you only because you value victory too
much. It is not the "great thing" that you believe to have achieved, even though you have
a right to your feelings. The great thing is that
there was something already present—and
you were allowed to substitute it in place of
your misconceptions—something true and
real. Without it your victory also would have

been a mere moral reaction without meaning. As it is, it has become a chapter in your life— your life, dear Mr. Kappus, I think of it with so many wishes for you.

Do you recall, from your childhood on, how very much this life of yours has longed for greatness? I see it now, how from the vantage point of greatness it longs for even greater greatness. That is why it does not let up being difficult, but that is also why it will not cease to grow.

If I were to tell you one more thing, it would be this: Do not believe that the one who seeks to comfort you lives without difficulty the simple and humble words that sometimes help you. His life contains much grief and sadness and he remains far behind you. Were it not so, he would not have found those words.

Yours,
Rainer Maria Rilke

9

"It is always my wish that you might find enough patience within yourself to endure, and enough innocence to have faith. . . . Believe me, life is right in all cases."

Furuborg, Jonsered, Sweden
4 November 1904

My dear Mr. Kappus,

During this time that has passed without a letter to you, I was traveling part of the time and partly so busy that I could not write. Even today writing is difficult, for before I could write your letter, I was obliged to write many others, so that my hand is tired. If dictating were possible, I would tell you so much. Instead, please accept just a few words as response to your long letter.

I think of you often, dear Mr. Kappus, and send you wishes with such concentration, that that itself should somehow help you. I am often in doubt that my letters can really be a help to you. Please don't answer with: Yes, they are! Just accept them without thanks and let us await what will happen.

It is probably not necessary to reply in detail to your letter. For what I could say to you about your inclination to doubt or about your inability to bring your inner and outer life into harmony, or about everything else that causes you concern—it is always that which I have already said: It is always my wish that you might find enough patience within yourself to endure, and enough innocence to have faith. It is my wish that you might gain more and more trust in whatever is difficult for you, in your aloneness, among other things. Allow life to happen to you. Believe me, life is right in all cases.

And about feelings: All feelings that integrate and inspire are pure. Impure is the feeling that touches only *one* side of your being and is tearing you up so. Everything you can think about in your childhood is good. Everything that causes you to be more than you have been in your best hours is right. Every advancement is good if it pervades your whole bloodstream, when it is not due to intoxication, not due to being conditioned to sadness, but to transparent joy. Do you understand what I mean?

Your doubt can become a good attribute if you *discipline* it. It must become a *knowing*; it must become the critic. Ask it, as often as it wishes to spoil something, why something is ugly. Demand proof of it, test it, and you will find it perhaps perplexed and confused, perhaps also in protest. But don't give in; demand arguments. Act with alertness and responsibility, each and every time, and the day will come when doubt will change from a destroyer to become one of your best fellow-workers, perhaps the wisest of all that have a part in building your life. That is all, dear Mr. Kappus, that I am able to say to you today. I shall under separate cover send you a small work that has appeared in Prague in the *Deutsche Arbeit*. In it I speak further to you of life and death and of how both are great and wonderful.

Yours,
Rainer Maria Rilke

10

"I can only wish that you trustingly and patiently allow that grand solitude to work in you. . . . It will act as an anonymous influence, akin to how ancestral blood constantly moves and merges with our own and links with that of the individual, never to be unlinked."

Paris
the day after Christmas, 1908

You should know, dear Franz, how happy I was to have received this beautiful letter of yours. The messages that you sent me, sincere and frankly expressed as they are again, were good news to me. The longer I thought about it, the more I felt them to be really good. I actually wanted to write this so that you could receive it by Christmas Eve; but because of the amount and variety of work with which I am living uninterruptedly this winter, good old Christmastime has approached so rapidly that I hardly had time to attend to the most necessary tasks, much less write. But I have thought of you often during these holidays and have imagined how tranquil you must be in your lonely fort between empty hills, attacked by great southern winds, as if they mean to devour them in large chunks.

The silence must be immense where there is space for such sounds and movements. And when one realizes that the presence of the distant sea and its melody is added to all this, perhaps as the innermost tone in this prehistoric harmony, then I can only wish that you trustingly and patiently allow that grand solitude to work in you. It is no longer possible to be erased from your life. It shall be imminent in all that you experience and all that you do. It will act as an anonymous influence, akin to how ancestral blood constantly moves and merges with our own and links with that of the individual, never to be unlinked. It is gently decisive at each crossroad of our life.

Yes, I am glad that you now have this certain, steady, safe career existence. This title, this uniform, this military service—all of

these tangible but restrictive things—in surroundings, with a small staff equally isolated,
take on a seriousness and an importance above
the usual playfulness, the waiting-for-the-
time-to-pass characteristic of the military career. This environment not only necessitates
vigilance in application, and allows for independent attentiveness to detail, but it actually
provides training for these qualities. To be in
circumstances that work in us, that place us
before great aspects of nature from time to
time, that is all we need.

Art also is only a way of life, and we can,
no matter how we live, and without knowing
it, prepare ourselves for it. With each encounter with truth one draws nearer to reaching
communion with it, more so than those in
unreal, half-artistic careers—by pretending
proximity to art, they actually deny and attack
the existence of all art. All those in the field of
journalism and nearly all critics do it, as well
as three-fourths of those engaged in literature,
or who wish to call it that. I am glad that you
have overcome the danger of being caught up

in such a realm, and that you are somewhere in a rugged reality alone and courageous.

May the year ahead of you keep and strengthen you in that resolve.

Always,
Yours,
Rainer Maria Rilke

About the Author

Rainer Maria Rilke was born in Prague, Czechoslovakia, in 1875. His father was an officer in the army, and he was at first sent to a military school. After that, largely on his own, he studied philosophy, history, literature, and art in Prague, Munich, and Berlin.

He started writing poetry at an early age, and became famous, first in Europe and then worldwide, for his poetry, novels, and letters. He traveled widely throughout Germany, Russia, France, Italy, Spain, Switzerland, Egypt, and Scandinavia.

He married Clara Westhoff in 1901, and had a daughter, Ruth, in 1902. After the birth of their daughter, they moved to Paris, where Clara worked with the famous sculptor

Auguste Rodin and Rilke wrote a monograph on him.

He died in France in 1926, and is buried beside the little church of Raron, overlooking the Rhone Valley.

About the Translator

Joan Marie Burnham was born in Berlin, Germany. She moved to Milwaukee, Wisconsin, at age ten and remained there until she graduated with honors from Milwaukee-Downer College (now Lawrence University) with majors in German and English.

Her postgraduate work consisted of study in Germany, where she earned a Masters Degree in Teaching of German from the University of Georgia.

She lives in Marin County, California.

About the Editor

Marc Allen is co-founder and president of New World Library. He is the author of several books, including *The Perfect Life* and *Tantra for the West—A Guide to Personal Freedom*. A musician and composer, he has recorded several albums. Allen lives in Marin County, California, where he divides his time between writing, music, and the publishing company.

The Classic Wisdom Collection
of
New World Library

New World Library is dedicated to publishing books and cassettes that help improve the quality of our lives.

For a catalog of our fine books and cassettes, contact:

New World Library
58 Paul Drive
San Rafael, CA 94903
Phone: (415) 472-2100
FAX: (415) 472-6131

Or call toll free:

(800) 227-3900
In Calif.: (800) 632-2122